AMERICA
THE BEAUTIFUL

Great God! we thank thee for this home —
This bounteous birthland of the free;
Where wanderers from afar may come,
And breathe the air of liberty!
Still may her flowers untrampled spring,
Her harvests wave, her cities rise;
And yet, till Time shall fold his wing,
Remain earth's loveliest paradise!

William Jewett Pabodic

ideals®

Ideals Publishing Corp.
Nashville, Tennessee

AMERICA *the* BEAUTIFUL

contents

*O*ur *A*rchitectural *H*eritage 4

*T*owns and *V*illages 20

*O*ur *C*ountry's *C*oastlines 40

*T*he *F*armlands 56

*I*nland *W*aters 68

*T*he *G*olden *W*est 82

*C*ountryside of the *S*outh 96

*M*ountain *R*anges 116

*H*awaii and *A*laska 134

*O*ur *N*ation's *P*arks and *M*onuments 140

ACKNOWLEDGMENTS

First and last two verses from *LINCOLN PORTRAIT* by Aaron Copland. Copyright 1943 by Aaron Copland, Renewed 1970. Reprinted by permission of Aaron Copland and Boosey & Hawkes, Inc., Sole Publishers and Licensees; PRAIRIE SPRING from *O PIONEERS!* by Willa Cather. Copyright 1913 and 1941 by Willa Sibert Cather. Reprinted by permission of Houghton Mifflin Company; THE MOUNTAIN CANYON from *THE ETERNAL THINGS* by Grace Noll Crowell. Copyright 1942 by Harper & Row, Publishers, Inc. Renewed 1970 by Reid Crowell. Reprinted by permission of Harper & Row, Publishers, Inc.; WILD HORSES from *POEMS OF INSPIRATION AND COURAGE* by Grace Noll Crowell. Copyright 1940 by Harper & Row, Publishers, Inc. Renewed 1968 by Grace Noll Crowell. Reprinted by permission of Harper & Row, Publishers, Inc.; THE GIFT OUTRIGHT, Copyright 1942 by Robert Frost and renewed 1970 by Lesley Frost Ballantine. Reprinted from *THE POETRY OF ROBERT FROST* edited by Edward Connery Lathem, by permission of Henry Holt and Company, Inc.; "THE NEW WORLD from *THE NEW WORLD* by Edgar Lee Masters. Copyright 1937 by Edgar Lee Masters. An Appleton-Century-Crofts/Hawthorn Book. Reprinted by permission of E.P. Dutton, A Division of NAL Penguin Inc." THE WESTERN SKY by Archibald MacLeish. Copyright ᶜ by Archibald MacLeish. Reprinted by permission of Houghton Mifflin Company; NOT LEARNED FROM BOOKS by Jessie Wilmore Murton. Used by permission of Pacific Press Publishing Association, Boise, ID; excerpt from *TOMORROW IS NOW* by Eleanor Roosevelt. Copyright ᶜ 1963 by the Estate of Anna Eleanor Roosevelt. Reprinted by permission of Harper & Row, Publishers, Inc.; THEY CALLED IT AMERICA by Rabbi Abba Hillel Silver from *SUNSHINE MAGAZINE*, July, 1966. Used by permission; excerpt from *TRAVELS WITH CHARLEY* by John Steinbeck. Copyright ᶜ 1961, 1962 by the Curtis Publishing Co., Inc. Copyright ᶜ 1962 by John Steinbeck. All rights reserved. Reprinted by permission of Viking Penguin Inc.; SIMPLE LOVELINESS by Gladys Taber. Copyright ᶜ 1964 by Family Circle, Inc. Used by permission of Brandt & Brandt Literary Agents, Inc. Our sincere thanks to the following whose addresses we were unable to locate: Mabel Law Atkinson for WITH FRIENDLY FOLK; the Estate of Annie Dodson Buck for BEYOND THE ROCKS; Marjorie Sharp Carter for TO THE GRAND CANYON; Rosa Mary Clausen-Mohr for MY LAND; Arnold J. Copeland for AMERICA, OUR HERITAGE; Jean M. Drum for AN UNKNOWN SHORE; Charles Johnson for THE NORTHWOODS; Evelyn Long for THE SOUTH IN THE SPRINGTIME from *WORTH REMEMBERING*, Copyright 1965 by Evelyn Long; Gelia K. Parker for JUST GOD . . . AND SKY . . . AND GREEN; T. M. Rutledge for MYSTIC RIVER; R. H. Sotherland for FROM OUT THE SOIL; the Estate of Nancy Byrd Turner for SEAWATER; Arthur J. Weber for TO LIVE BY THE SEA; Ralph M. J. Worth for IT'S SPRING.

Cover Photo
SNOQUALMIE NATIONAL FOREST
WASHINGTON
Jeff Gnass

Photo Opposite
BALD EAGLE
D & P Valenti
H. Armstrong Roberts, Inc.

SAN XAVIER DEL BAC MISSION
TUCSON, ARIZONA
H. Armstrong Roberts, Inc.

O beautiful for spacious skies,
For amber waves of grain,

The Gift Outright

Robert Frost

The land was ours before we were the land's.
She was our land more than a hundred years
Before we were her people. She was ours
In Massachusetts, in Virginia,
But we were England's, still colonials,
Possessing what we still were unpossessed by,
Possessed by what we now no more possessed.
Something we were withholding made us weak
Until we found out that it was ourselves
We were withholding from our land of living,
And forthwith found salvation in surrender.
Such as we were we gave ourselves outright
(The deed of gift was many deeds of war)
To the land vaguely realizing westward,
But still unstoried, artless, unenhanced,
Such as she was, such as she would become.

Just God
and Sky
and Green

Gelia K. Parker

I'd love to live in a forest room
With moss beneath my feet,
And the ceiling made of leafy green
Where boughs of pine trees meet.

The lighting I'd like indirect—
Just sunlight trickling through,
And here and there between the leaves,
A patch of heaven's blue.

Oh, I'd love a little forest room
With walls of roughened bark,
And my only entertainment
Just the sweet song of a lark.

I'd let the whole world pass me by
And live a life serene,
With all the things I'd ever need—
Just God and sky and green.

Photo Opposite
CAMBRIDGE, MARYLAND
Tom Algire
FPG International

Photo Overleaf
GOLDEN GATE BRIDGE
CALIFORNIA
Jeff Gnass

Homecoming Streets

Helen Harrington

The streets are calling all their people home;
Lights leap up, and smoke from poked-up fires
Signals excitedly to those who roam.
Every house, now, perking up, attires
Itself in what will have the most appeal
For hungry husbands, famished boys and girls;
Scents of roasts and vegetables that steal
Out kitchen windows, pie fragrance that curls
Down walks. Almost everything has been done
To make the welcome felt and will be
Complete and right when the returning one
Is met beyond the threshold tenderly
By what all homeward bound have right to know . . .
A shining smile and a glad hello!

PRIVATE PLEASE
DO NOT ENTER

The Homestead

Lady Spencer

It is not as it used to be
When you and I were young,
When round each elm and maple tree
The honeysuckles clung;

But still I love the cottage where
I passed my early years,
Though not a single face is there
That memory endears.

It is not as it used to be!
The moss is on the roof,
And from their nests beneath the eaves
The swallows keep aloof.

The robins—how they used to sing
When you and I were young;
And how did flit the wild bee's wing
The opening flowers among!

It is not as it used to be!
The voices loved of yore,
And the forms that we were wont to see,
We see and hear no more.

No more! Alas, we look in vain,
For those to whom we clung,
And loved as we can love but once,
When you and I were young.

Photo Opposite
CARSON HOUSE
CALIFORNIA
Josef Muench

Photo Overleaf
JACKSON, NEW HAMPSHIRE
Ed Cooper

Towns and VILLAGES

PENN'S LANDING
PENNSYLVANIA
H. Armstrong Roberts, Inc.

For purple mountain majesties
Above the fruited plain.

Simple Loveliness

Gladys Taber

One reason for the beauty of New England has always been the architecture, for the houses and churches were built to fit the land and the climate. The steep pitch of roofs shed heavy snow, low eaves shed the melt easily, and the small-paned windows kept out the bitter cold, as did the low-hung doors. The houses were as staunch as the sailing ships that went out from Gloucester, New Bedford, Provincetown. There was no gingerbread decoration. But the fanlights over front doors had grace; and the shutters, that could be locked when needed, gave design to the plain houses. In the Victorian period some of the beautiful dwellings were "done over"— with unfortunate results. Now owners tend to remove the ugly porches and fretwork, bringing the houses back to simple loveliness.

Photo Opposite
RESIDENT TRUMAN HOME
MISSOURI
FPG International

Photo Overleaf
WILMINGTON, DELAWARE
Gene Ahrens

The Hometown

Edgar A. Guest

It doesn't matter much
Be its buildings great or small,
The hometown, the hometown
Is the best town, after all.

The cities of the millions
Have the sun and stars above,
But they lack the friendly faces
Of the few you've learned to love.

And with all their pomp of riches
And with all their teeming throngs,
The heart of man is rooted
In the town where he belongs.

There are places good to visit,
There are cities fair to see,
There are haunts of charm and beauty
Where at times it's good to be,

But the humblest little hamlet
Sings a melody to some,
And no matter where they travel
It is calling them to come;

Though cities rise to greatness
And are gay with gaudy dress,
There is something in the hometown
Which no other towns possess.

The hometown has a treasure
Which the distance cannot gain,
It is there the hearts are kindest,
There the gentlest friends remain;

It is there a mystic something
Seems to permeate the air,
To set the weary wanderer
To wishing he were there;

And be it great or humble,
It still holds mankind in thrall,
For the hometown, the hometown
Is the best town after all.

Photo Opposite
AMHERST, NEW HAMPSHIRE
Fred Sieb

The Hills of New England

Earle J. Grant

Have you been to the hills of New England
When Spring was scattering gay daffodils
And, piercing the crystalline air,
You could hear the bluebird's trills?

Have you been to the hills of New England
When Summer was draping roses of red
Up pillar and post of each cozy cottage
And hanging white satin clouds overhead?

Have you been to the hills of New England
When God's artist, Autumn, was painting trees
In hues rich and rare, from crimson to gold,
And scents of ripe apples were riding the breeze?

Have you been to the hills of New England
When Winter was whirling white flakes of snow
From the pearl-gray heights of the heavens
To frost the waiting earth below?

Photo Opposite
EAST ORANGE, VERMONT
Gene Ahrens

Photo Overleaf
MORRISTOWN, NEW JERSEY
Gene Ahrens

Freedom

Clara Smith Reber

Freedom is a breath of air,
Pine-scented, or salty like the sea;
Freedom is a field new-plowed . . .
Furrows of democracy!

Freedom is a forest,
Trees tall and straight as men.
Freedom is a printing press . . .
The power of the pen!

Freedom is a country church,
A cathedral's stately spire;
Freedom is a spirit
That can set the soul on fire!

Freedom is man's birthright,
A sacred, living rampart;
The pulsebeat of humanity . . .
The throb of a nation's heart!

Photo Opposite
STOCKBRIDGE, MASSACHUSETTS
A. A. Trimels

With Friendly Folk

Mabel Law Atkinson

I love a country town with friendly folk
Whose wealth of human kindness all may own;
Where all are neighbors; where the heavy yoke,
The cross of sorrow, is not borne alone.

In country skies, contentment's rainbow glows
To glorify the rugged path of toil.
And maple hills reecho glad "hellos";
Peace fills the hearts of tillers of the soil.

I love a country town; with tenderness
Its gentle arms enfold me and its smile
Is like an ever lingering caress—
An atmosphere that bids me feel worthwhile.

The light of love upon its cheerful face,
A country town is such a friendly place.

A Picture of a Village

Loise Pinkerton Fritz

There's a picture of a village
In a valley that I know,
Where the moon is shining brightly
On the newly fallen snow;
Where the air is crisp and frosty
And the night's clear as a bell;
And the evergreens are snow-tipped
On the hills and in the dell.

There's a picture of a village
In a valley that I love,
Where the snow-clad housetops glisten
Like the stars that shine above.
There's a beam that lights the pathway
From one doorstep to the next—
It's the special glow of friendliness
In the village I love best.

There's a picture of a village
In a valley dear to me,
And embellishing this picture
Is the frame of memory.

Photo Opposite
VILLAGE AT DUSK
WESTFIELD, CONNECTICUT
H. Armstrong Roberts, Inc.

LIGHTHOUSE IN MAINE
Damm/Zefa
H. Armstrong Roberts, Inc.

America! America!
God shed His grace on thee,
And crown thy good with brotherhood
From sea to shining sea.

An Unknown Shore

Jean M. Drum

As I stand on beautiful white beaches
And look with awe across the wide span of ocean,
I know a peace
Never felt anywhere else.

I marvel at palm trees
Swaying gently in the breeze.
I see the hand of the Creator
In the shells upon the sand.

I watch with wide-eyed wonder
As the white lace-edged waves
Rush to caress the shores,
Then swiftly descend once more.

My heart soars with the sea gull,
And I long to sail away,
To explore an unknown shore
Far across this unknown sea.

My Land

Rosa Mary Clausen-Mohr

This is my land, my glorious land—
Its forest wealth, its prairie sand,
Its lakes of blue and green and gray
Where weary people holiday;
Its winding waters which search the sea,
Reflecting hill and cloud and tree;
Its wide expanse of spacious plain
With seas of green and golden grain;
Its purple mountains towering high
Into a height of cloud and sky.
Created by our Father's hand,
He gave to us this wondrous land;
Yes, free to worship and free to roam,
Blest are we who call this home.

Photo Opposite
EGRET
FLORIDA
H. Armstrong Roberts, In

By the Sea

Arthur J. Weber

To live by the sea
is to hear the sound
of time and eternity;
to hear the soft whisper
of the water washing
the sand of the shore,
gently swaying
the moments of time;
or to hear the hard slap
of the whitecap
upon the rock, loudly
speaking the eons
of eternity . . . .
This is to live
by the sea.

Photo Opposite
PACIFIC GROVE, CALIFORNIA
Fred Sieb

Seawater

Nancy Byrd Turner

There's an old light in seawater,
An ancient beauty drawn
From many a coral sunset
And many an opal dawn,

From the green of shadowed shorelands
And the blue of tranquil skies . . .
There's an old light in seawater
That is good for weary eyes.

There's an old song in seawater,
An everlasting tale
That great tides tell, returning,
Of love that shall not fail,

Of patience that endureth
For all the ages long. . . .
I have cleansed my soul in seawater,
And now I shall be strong.

Windmills

Henry David Thoreau

The most foreign and picturesque structures on the Cape, to an inlander, not excepting the saltworks, are the windmills—gray-looking, octagonal towers, with long timbers slanting to the ground in the rear, and there resting on a cartwheel, by which their fans are turned round to face the wind. These appeared also to serve in some measure for props against its force. A great circular rut was worn around the building by the wheel. [The windmills] looked loose and slightly locomotive, like huge wounded birds, trailing a wing or a leg, and reminded one of pictures of the Netherlands.

Being on elevated ground, and high in themselves, they serve as landmarks, for there are no tall trees, or other objects commonly, which can be seen at a distance in the horizon; though the outline of the land itself is so firm and distinct, that an insignificant cone, or even precipice of sand, is visible at a great distance from over the sea. Sailors making the land commonly steer either by the windmills, or the meeting houses. In the country, we are obliged to steer by the meeting houses alone. Yet the meeting house is a kind of windmill, which runs one day in seven, turned either by the winds of doctrine or public opinion, or more rarely by the winds of Heaven, where another sort of grist is ground, of which, if it be not all bran or musty, if it be not *plaster,* we trust to make bread of life.

Photo Opposite
CAPE COD, MASSACHUSETTS
Fred Sieb

New England Harbor

Joy Belle Burgess

The breeze is fresh with salt sea air
Where anchored boats in stillness lie.
Where wharves are spread with fishing nets,
A sea gull lifts its lonely cry.

The pearly shells upon the sand
Are tumbled by the sweeping tide,
While here beyond the restless surf
A helpless boat lies on its side.

The silver waves come murmuring
Against the quaint old weathered pier,
Where fragments of a dream and song
Revive a scene of yesteryear.

And peace is steeped in warm content
When long and slumberous hours have flown . . .
When fishing boats upon the sea
At last come gently, safely home.

THE FARMLANDS

ELVIRA, IOWA
Gene Ahrens

O beautiful for pilgrim feet,
Whose stern, impassioned stress

From Out the Soil

R. H. Sotherland

Looking backward across the fields
As the sun drops in the west,
The farmer, tired but happy,
Turns toward home and needed rest.
First the faithful horses
Must be groomed with proper care,
Given refreshing drink and best of food.
For man, they did their share.

Tilling the ground and planting the seed,
Working from dawn until dark;
The creaking harness, the strain upon
  chain
To the song of the meadowlark,
The only sound that reaches man's ear
As he plods through the heat of the day;
He feels the touch of the hand of God
As he reverently bows to pray.

The life-giving seed, the fields well tilled,
He awaits and welcomes the showers;
He witnesses the miracle of creation,
In the warmth of the summer hours.
He sees fields of golden grain
Moving at the slightest breeze,
Reflecting the rays of the noonday sun,
Turning the whole into enchanted seas.

Contentedly he rests until the harvest
  moon
Calls him once again to the fields;
It is then he reaps a just reward
As he harvests what the good earth yields
God expects us to do our part;
We cannot reap without toil,
But doing our share as man should do . . .
Great gifts come from out the soil.

Prairie Spring

Willa Cather

Evening and the flat land,
Rich and somber and always silent;
The miles of fresh-plowed soil,
Heavy and black, full of strength and harshness;
The growing wheat, the growing weeds,
The toiling horses, the tired men;
The long empty roads,
Sullen fires of sunset, fading,
The eternal, unresponsive sky.
Against all this, Youth,
Flaming like the wild roses,
Singing like the larks over the plowed fields,
Flashing like a star out of the twilight;
Youth with its insupportable sweetness,
Its fierce necessity,
Its sharp desire,
Singing and singing,
Out of the lips of silence,
Out of the earthy dusk.

Photo Opposite
INDIANA FARMLAND
Bob Clemenz

Land of Gold

Arnold J. Copeland

America, our heritage, thou land of golden fields,
Where ev'ry fertile valley a fruitful harvest yields,
Fair land of lofty mountains, of forest, stream, and lake,
Vast industries, great cities, no foe shall ever take.

How manifold thy blessings! How priceless our estate
To foster hope and brotherhood, to ban discord and hate!
From wilderness to nation thy sons have seen thee rise,
One mighty federation, where none dare tyrannize.

On guard, then, O America! Let nothing ever dim
The flame of true democracy, nor still the fervent hymn
Of liberty and justice and noble destiny.
Again we raise our thanks to God, America, for thee.

Photo Opposite
WISCONSIN FARMLAND
J. Zimmerman
FPG International

Photo Overleaf
ST. NICHOLAS, MINNESOTA
Grant Heilman

*I*NLAND WATERS

HARPERS FERRY,
WEST VIRGINIA
Gene Ahrens

A thoroughfare for freedom beat
Across the wilderness.

Beyond the Rocks

Annie Dodson Buck

There was calmness and nature
At her best here,
As I sat near the ocean's edge,
My thoughts free;

Gazing at the wide expanse,
With lighthouse near,
Beyond the rocks there was
Depth and mystery!

A galaxy of fragrant blossoms
Were there to greet one;
White daisies, bluebells, and
Many more.

Nearby was the cottage,
One very neat,
Where one knew the joy of dwelling
Near the shore.

Overhead the limitless blue sky,
Also the ocean blue,
Fleecy clouds on review;
At my feet shells from the sea.

The subdued lap of the waves
Was light music, true,
But beyond the rocks
Symphonies were playing for me!

This Is Our Country

George H. Brubach

It's wonderful, this country we're proud to call ours
With its marvelous landscapes and exotic flowers.

The rugged mountains, their snowcapped peaks
And tortuous, surging, tumbling creeks.

Its caverns and canyons, the high waterfalls,
Magnificent redwoods, massive and tall.

Its wide green valleys, the rivers and lakes . . .
God's great gifts, for all to partake.

This is America from sea to sea,
And we'll give our lives to keep it free.

May its flag be our emblem of peace and tranquillity,
A banner of freedom for you and for me.

This is our country; it's yours and mine . . . .
May we love and protect it till the end of time.

Photo Opposite
ILLINOIS RIVER
TAHLEQUAH, OKLAHOMA
Bob Taylor

The Lighthouse

Becky Jennings

The mighty lighthouse stands secure,
Undaunted by the restless sea;
Ravaged by the changing tides
And buffeted by winds blown free.

Yet, it sheds its beacon straight and true,
Unfaltering in the bleakest night,
Guiding every passing ship
Uncertain of the course that's right.

May we be diligent and true,
Dedicated to the right
And like the stalwart lighthouse stand
A beacon in the darkest night.

Photo Opposite
LIGHTHOUSE
SANDUSKY, OHIO
Ken Dequaine

Photo Overleaf
MISSISSIPPI RIVER
IOWA
J. Blank
H. Armstrong Roberts, Inc.

Not Learned from Books

Jessie Wilmore Murton

There are some things we did not learn from books . . . the thicket where the bobwhites build their nest . . . the hillside where we always found the best and sweetest wild strawberries . . . and the nooks where pale arbutus trailed.

We found the crooks of trees most comfortable in which to sit . . . and feasted richly without benefit of printed page or recipes or cooks.

There are so many things not taught in school . . . how best to make a willow whistle sing . . . the shape of stones for skipping on a pool . . . the secret ways of tree and fin and wing.

One soon forgets the facts that pages yield . . . but not the wisdom of the brook and field.

Photo Opposite
WHITE RIVER
CALICO ROCK, ARKANSAS
Arkansas Dept. of Parks and Tourism

Photo Overleaf
LAKE TAHOE
NEVADA
Gene Ahrens

CHISOS MOUNTAINS
BIG BEND NATIONAL PARK
TEXAS
Tom Algire

Photo Overleaf
TIN MOUNTAIN
DEATH VALLEY, CALIFORNIA
Ed Cooper
H. Armstrong Roberts, Inc.

America! America!
God mend thine every flaw,
Confirm thy soul in self-control,
Thy liberty in law.

Principles on Which this Nation Is Based

Eleanor Roosevelt

It is essential to turn back to our history now and then to remind ourselves of the principles on which this nation is based. . . .We could never have conquered the wilderness; never have built the foundations of a country and a new concept of life, based on the fullest and freest development of the individual; never have overcome vast difficulties and dangers, if we had not had a new idea, an idea so noble in concept that it gave us confidence in ourselves and gave us the strength to build this new nation, step by step.

Photo Opposite
TOADSTOOL STATE PARK
NEBRASKA
Gene Ahrens

Photo Overleaf
GRAND CANYON NATIONAL PARK
ARIZONA
Jeff Gnass

To the Grand Canyon

Marjorie Sharp Carter

Vast, blue-shadowed pinnacles, awesome and still
With dreaming sun-peaks on each violet hill,
Enraptured with majesty's beauty, we thrill
To your ancient magnificent colors, sublime!
You are long eons old, almost older than time—
A rose and gold glory—above reason and rhyme.

Your river's knife-silver thread, from afar—
Bright angels still guard you—time never shall mar
Your pageant of colors, beneath sun and star.
This rock-silent grandeur of time-gorged levee
Is a huge panorama all poets should see
To teach us that time is eternity.

The New World

Edgar Lee Masters

This America is an ancient land,
Conquered and re-conquered by successive races.
It is the Radiant Land and Continent of the Blest
Forever won and forever lost,
And forever seen by that vision which thrilled Balboa
Staring the Pacific;
And forever seen by that revelation of the soul
Which came to John Keats through Homer,
For both seas and land, and visions of a new day
   may be seen,
And gold may be seen by Cortes and Pizarro
   and their sons,
Who turn all Radiant Lands to gold, and starve therefore.
But this New World is forever new to hands
   that keep it new.

Photo Opposite
CARLSBAD CAVERNS
NEW MEXICO
Gene Ahrens

COUNTRYSIDE *of the* SOUTH

ORTON PLANTATION GARDENS
WILMINGTON, NORTH CAROLINA
Monserrate Schwartz

O beautiful for patriot dream
That sees beyond the years,

It's Spring

Ralph M. J. Worth

The reeds have ceased their rattling sound
And tracks appear in softened ground;
The whistling of the peepers brings
The entrance of an early spring.
Now pushing up the meadow's edge
Are crocuses beneath the hedge;
A million buds are coming out,
Forsythia blooming all about.
A sense of kinship swiftly brings
A love for all these growing things,
And in the doorway where I stand,
Enchanted by the greening land,
With all the riches of a king,
My heart cries out,
"It's spring, it's spring!"

Photo Opposite
GUSTON HALL
LORTON, VIRGINI
FPG Internationa

The South in the Springtime

Evelyn Long

The South in the springtime is a bright carnival
Of flowers on a carpet of green neath a sky of blue;
An apple, plum, and peach blossom festival;
An endless trail of azaleas in every vivid hue.

White dogwood, pink camellias, sweet honeysuckle,
Roses, magnolia, and bridal wreaths abundantly grow
Where the petals of lavender crepe myrtle,
When fallen, weave an intricate blanket of purple snow.

Photo Opposite
ALABAMA
Ken Dequaine

Green Things Growing

Dinah Maria Mulock

Oh, the green things growing, the green things growing,
The faint, sweet smell of the green things growing!
I should like to live, whether I smile or grieve,
Just to watch the happy life of my green things growing.

Oh, the fluttering and the pattering of those green things
    growing!
How they talk to each other, when none of us are knowing,
In the wonderful white of the weird moonlight
Or the dim dreamy dawn when the cocks are crowing.

I love, I love them so . . . my green things growing!
And I think that they love me, without false showing;
For by many a tender touch, they comfort me so much,
With the soft mute comfort of green things growing.

Photo Opposite
MIDDLETON GARDE
SOUTH CAROLINA
FPG International

Nature

Henry David Thoreau

O nature! I do not aspire
To be the highest in thy choir,
To be a meteor in thy sky,
Or comet that may range on high;
Only a zephyr that may blow
Among the reeds by the river low;
Give me thy most privy place
Where to run my airy race.

In some withdrawn, unpublic mead
Let me sigh upon a reed,
Or in the woods, with leafy din,
Whisper the still evening in;
Some still work give me to do,
Only, be it near to you!

For I'd rather be thy child
And pupil, in the forest wild,
Than be the king of men elsewhere,
And most sovereign slave of care;
To have one moment of thy dawn,
Than share the city's year forlorn.

Wild Horses

Grace Noll Crowell

Sometimes, across this land of silver grasses,
There comes a sound upon the listening air
As if, along the old dim trails and passes,
Horses were there,
Galloping swiftly, riderless, unbidden,
Their smoky manes a blur against the light,
Wild horses that have never yet been ridden,
Lunging in fright
Before some scent or sound, some windward gleaning
Of distant threat, their arching necks held high,
Their ears alert to catch the inner meaning
Of step or cry . . . .

Almost I see them down the windy weather,
Their satin muscles rippling as they run,
Wild horses that have never known a tether,
Mates to the sun,
Mates to the lightning and the crashing thunder,
The black-winged night, the white onrushing dawn—
Wild horses—Ah, the beauty and the wonder
Of things long gone!

Photo Opposite
PARIS PARK
FAYETTE COUNTY, KENTUCKY
FPG International

Photo Overleaf
MYNELLE GARDENS
JACKSON, MISSISSIPPI
Gene Ahrens

No Lovelier Place

Earle J. Grant

I know of no lovelier place on earth
Than the South when the fragile blossoming
Of peach and pear and plum is brought to birth
Upon greening hills by the warmth of spring.
Nor could there be a fairer sight to see
Than violets trimming her crystal streams
While dogwoods spread their white embroidery
And the redbuds thrill us with cerise gleams.
Silver satin clouds drift in turquoise skies,
Birds become ecstatic with songs of praise;
Up from valleys, amethystine mists rise,
And azaleas pink-fringe the woodland ways.
Surely no one could ever ask for more
Than the South with white lilacs at the door.

Photo Oppos
LOUISIAN
Ed Coope

Woodland Scenery

Washington Irving

There is a serene and settled majesty in woodland scenery that enters into the soul, and delights and elevates it, and fills it with noble inclinations. As the leaves of trees are said to absorb all noxious qualities of the air and to breathe forth a purer atmosphere, so it seems to me as if they drew from us all sordid and angry passions, and breathed forth peace and philanthropy.

There is something nobly simple and pure in a taste for the cultivation of forest trees. It argues, I think, a sweet and generous nature to have this strong relish for the beauties of vegetation and this friendship for the hardy and glorious sons of the forest. There is a grandeur of thought connected with this part of rural economy. It is, if I may be allowed the figure, the heroic line of husbandry. It is worthy of liberal, and freeborn, and aspiring men. He who plants an oak looks forward to future ages, and plants for posterity. Nothing can be less selfish than this.

Photo Opposite
GREENFIELD GARDENS
NORTH CAROLINA
Dick Smith

For You, O Democracy

Walt Whitman

Come, I will make the continent indissoluble,
I will make the most splendid race the sun ever shone
    upon.
I will make divine magnetic lands,
With the love of comrades,
With the lifelong love of comrades.

I will plant companionship thick as trees along all the rivers
    of America, and along the shores of the great lakes,
    and all over the prairies,
I will make inseparable cities with their arms about each
    other's necks,
By the love of comrades,
By the manly love of comrades.

For you these from me, O Democracy, to serve you,
For you, for you I am trilling these songs.

Photo Opposite
NORTH CAROLINA
Ken Dequaine

MOUNTAIN RANGES

GRAND TETON NATIONAL PARK
WYOMING
Camerique

Thine alabaster cities gleam,
Undimmed by human tears.

The Northwoods

Charles Johnson

Not far to the north, where your soul is free,
Remote and aloof in its majesty,
Lies a spot where God has taken a hand
To create a beautiful wonderland.
He sent dew and rain from heaven above
To form crystal lakes we dearly love.
Seed and pollen were borne on the breeze
To produce a forest of lovely trees.

Then animals and birds of every hue
Were added that we might listen, too.
The wild melody of the northwoods in tune,
The eerie cry of the mating loon,
The chirp of the spring frogs in swampland near,
The call of the eagle sharp and clear.

The approach of the graceful doe and fawn—
Watch in awed silence, for soon they are gone.
See the sunset glory of purple and gold
As the arms of twilight the earth enfold.
Watch the heavens bloom with countless stars,
Then fade as northern lights sweep in bars.

It gives you a feeling pure and clear;
Surely God is very near.

The Mountain Canyon

Grace Noll Crowell

Here is such dark cool beauty, such clear sound:
An echo runs along the far-off heights
Like crystal striking crystal. Seaward bound
The mountain torrent, filled with silver lights,
Makes wild protest; and a trodden twig somewhere
Breaks, and the sound is loud upon the air.

An aspen quakes beside a waterfall.
The pines climb skyward, not a branch is stirred;
The blue spruce lifts against the canyon wall,
And now a dark bough dips where a crimson bird
With iridescent wings and breast of flame
Swings, and calls to his mate a singing name.

Deep in a dark cool tree a fiery bird
Has written a poem without pen or word.

Photo Opposite
PARADISE VALLEY
MONTANA
Larry Burton

Solitude

Shirley Sallay

I often long for mountains,
High, majestic, and cool,
Capped with deep eternal snow
And watered by a crystal pool.

I'd wander deep within their shade
And seek a spot to rest,
A place where I could dream a dream
Or solve some pressing quest.

But mountains are all far away,
There are none near to find—
And to my small rose garden
Those dreams are all confined.

I hope some day to journey
Far off into the hill,
There to taste of solitude
And all my dreams fulfill.

Photo Opposite
TIMPANOGOS
UTAH
Josef Muench

Photo Overleaf
AND TETONS
WYOMING
Larry Burton

My Walk Took Me Far

Joy Belle Burgess

The woods have been touched by the wintry air,
And, lo, what a glistening white splendor everywhere,
Stirring only by the whisper of falling flakes
And the murmuring sound the easy wind makes.

I feel the scrutiny of every eye
That peers from within the log and the limb so high,
And yet I dare to crunch my way
Step by step into their hideaway,

And to treasure the moments all my own,
To be awed by the hallowed calm, ere winter has flown;
To capture and cherish as the rapture unfolds,
The stillness that prevails, the beauty untold.

The fir boughs bend neath their ermine capes,
Barren limbs being clothed by each downy flake;
The icy little creek seeks out a way
Past drifts and white rocks, lest it go astray.

And ever the falling of the starry flakes
Piles drifts high, forming marvelous shapes.
Tall spindly towers, where young saplings stand,
And smooth white mounds mask brush o'er the land.

The woods have been touched by the wintry air,
And I alone know the peace, the beauty that is there;
For my walk took me far, far out into the cold,
Where winter spread her treasures for me to behold!

Psalm 121

I will lift up mine eyes unto the hills, from whence cometh my help.

My help cometh from the Lord, which made heaven and earth.

He will not suffer thy foot to be moved: he that keepeth thee will not slumber.

Behold, he that keepeth Israel shall neither slumber nor sleep.

The Lord is thy keeper: the Lord is thy shade upon thy right hand.

The sun shall not smite thee by day, nor the moon by night.

The Lord shall preserve thee from all evil: he shall preserve thy soul.

The Lord shall preserve thy going out and thy coming in from this time forth, and even for evermore.

Psalm 121

Travels with Charley

John Steinbeck

My plan was clear, concise, and reasonable, I think. For many years I have traveled in many parts of the world. In America I live in New York, or dip into Chicago or San Francisco. But New York is no more America than Paris is France or London is England. Thus I discovered that I did not know my own country. I, an American writer, writing about America, was working from memory, and the memory is at best a faulty, warpy reservoir. I had not heard the speech of America, smelled the grass and trees and sewage, seen its hills and water, its color and quality of light. I knew the changes only from books and newspapers. But more than this, I had not felt the country for twenty-five years. In short, I was writing of something I did not know about, and it seems to me that in a so-called writer this is criminal. My memories were distorted by twenty-five intervening years.

Once I traveled about in an old bakery wagon, double-doored rattler with a mattress on its floor. I stopped where people stopped or gathered, I listened and looked and felt, and in the process had a picture of my country the accuracy of which was impaired only by my own shortcomings.

So it was that I determined to look again, to try to rediscover this monster land. Otherwise, in writing, I could not tell the small diagnostic truths which are the foundations of the larger truth. . . .

Photo Opposite
ADIRONDACK STATE PARK
NEW YORK
Tom Algire

Photo Overleaf
MT. SHUKSAN
WASHINGTON
George Schwartz

LILIOUKALANI GARDENS
HAWAII
Bob Clemenz

America! America!
God shed His grace on thee,
And crown thy good with brotherhood
From sea to shining sea.

Mystic River

T. M. Rutledge

Mystic river, golden river,
Sun-made jewels form thy crown,
Captor of sun's ardent kisses
Clothed in heaven's azure gown.
Majestic waters, proudly flowing
On thy journey to the sea,
Keeper of Time's untold secrets,
Share thy mysteries with me.

Mystic river, silvery river,
In moon-made magic thou art dressed;
Music of thy murmuring ripples
Lullaby for a dreamer's rest.
Shimmering waters, softly wooing
Molten moonglow's liquid beams,
Beckoning for me to enter
Lonesome lands of life's lost dreams.

Mystic river, peaceful river,
Naught of strife or greed is there;
Sing to me of calm green valleys,
Silent hills, and woodlands fair.
Tranquil waters, gently flowing—
Placid, while we mortals grope,
Sing thy song of faith and courage,
Sing of everlasting hope.

Photo Opposite
KAUAI HONOPU FALLS
HAWAII
Ed Cooper

Photo Overleaf
MT. HUNTER
ALASKA
Ed Cooper

OUR NATION'S PARKS *and* MONUMENTS

WASHINGTON MONUMENT
WASHINGTON, D.C.
Jack Zehrt

Photo Overleaf
THE BADLANDS
THEODORE ROOSEVELT NAT'L PARK
NORTH DAKOTA
Jeff Gnass

America! America!
God shed His grace on thee,
And crown thy good with brotherhood
From sea to shining sea.

Lincoln Portrait

Aaron Copland

"Fellow citizens, we cannot escape history."
That is what he said,
That is what Abraham Lincoln said:
"Fellow citizens, we cannot escape history.
"We of this Congress and this administration will be
remembered in spite of ourselves. No personal significance
or insignificance can spare one or another of us.
"The fiery trial through which we pass will light us down,
in honor or dishonor, to the latest generation.
We—even here—hold the power and bear the responsibility."

Abe Lincoln was a quiet and a melancholy man.
But when he spoke of democracy,
This is what he said: he said:
"As I would not be a slave, so I would not be a master.
This expresses my idea of democracy.
Whatever differs from this, to the extent of the difference,
is no democracy."

Abraham Lincoln, sixteenth President of these United
States, is everlasting in the memory of his countrymen, for
on the battleground at Gettysburg, this is what he said:
This is what Abe Lincoln said:
"That from these honored dead we take increased devotion
to that cause for which they gave the last full
measure of devotion:
that we here highly resolve that these dead
shall not have died in vain: that this nation, under God,
shall have a new birth of freedom;
and that the government of the people, by the people,
for the people, shall not perish from the earth."

Photo Opposite
LINCOLN MEMORIAL
WASHINGTON, D.C.
Fred Sieb

AS IN THE HEARTS OF THE PEOPLE
FOR WHOM HE SAVED THE UNION
THE MEMORY OF ABRAHAM LINCOLN
IS ENSHRINED FOREVER

An Inestimable Jewel

Abraham Lincoln

It is not merely for today but for all time to come that we should perpetuate for our children's children that great and free government which we have enjoyed all our lives. I beg you to remember this, not merely for my sake, but for yours. I happen, temporarily, to occupy the White House. I am a living witness that any one of your children may look to come here as my father's child has. It is in order that each one of you may have, through this free government which we have enjoyed, an open field and a fair chance for your industry, enterprise, and intelligence that you may all have equal privileges in the race of life, with all its desirable human aspirations. It is for this the struggle should be maintained that we may not lose our birthright—not only for one, but for two or three years. The nation is worth fighting for to secure such an inestimable jewel.

A Nation's Strength

Ralph Waldo Emerson

What makes a nation's pillars high
And its foundations strong?
What makes it mighty to defy
The foes that round it throng?

It is not gold. Its kingdoms grand
Go down in battle shock;
Its shafts are laid on sinking sand,
Not on abiding rock.

Is it the sword? Ask the red dust
Of empires passed away;
The blood has turned their stones to rust,
Their glory to decay.

And is it pride? Ah, that bright crown
Has seemed to nations sweet;
But God has struck its luster down
In ashes at his feet.

Not gold but only men can make
A people great and strong;
Men who for truth and honor's sake
Stand fast and suffer long.

Brave men who work while others sleep,
Who dare while others fly. . . .
They build a nation's pillars deep
And lift them to the sky.

The Western Sky

Archibald MacLeish

Stand, stand against the rising night,
O freedom's land, O freedom's air:
Stand steep and keep the fading light
That eastward darkens everywhere.

Hold, hold the golden light and lift
Hill after hilltop, one by one—
Lift up America, O lift
Green freedom to the evening sun.

Lift up your hills till conquered men
Look westward to their blazing height:
Lift freedom till its fire again
Kindles the countries of the night.

Be proud, America, to bear
The endless labor of the free—
To strike for freedom everywhere
And everywhere bear liberty.

Lift up, O land, O land lift clear
The lovely signal of your skies.
If freedom darkens eastward here,
Here on the west let freedom rise.

Forest Cathedral

Olive Weaver Ridenour

No great cathedral here,
Except the trees
That touch the sky, and bring
Me to my knees
In reverential awe.

The only choir
Is that of singing birds;
Their songs inspire
My heart to sing the praise
Of Him who made
Each tree that towers so high,
Each tiny blade.

There is no altar here
Except the sod,
But . . . in this quiet place
My soul finds God!

Among Dakota's Hills

Frank Manhart

No crumbling stone—no mellow rock
The sculptor seeks where to reveal
The foremost men of hardy stock
Who served their country with rare zeal.

Among Dakota's hills so grand
The storms of time that never cease
Touch lightly mighty crags that stand
Where Borglum carves his masterpiece!

What if stone is a toilsome page?
How could a truly mindful son
Forget in this the golden age
The blessings the brave fathers won?

Look up, all you patriots true!
Where once the bare rock outward spread.
There valiant men have come in view.
Their deeds still live—they are not dead.

Our Washington warns of foreign foe,
Who would assail our shores again;
While Jefferson would have us know
That tyrants rise 'mongst thoughtless men.

Our Lincoln pleads for greater faith
In boundless power of the right
To hold intact the Ship of State,
And overcome opposing might.

There's Roosevelt who could inspire
His fellow man to seek high goals,
And hold to a wholesome desire,
And not to plead for grants and doles.

O Carver of the Noble Brow,
Hath ever other dreamer known
Such inspiration as yours now
To carve life into lifeless stone?

This I Believe

Helen Virden

I believe in the miracle of America . . .
In the common purpose of her people,
Their common hope and their common devotion.
My faith evades definition,
But it is built on Plymouth Rock,
Concord Bridge, and Valley Forge.

I reaffirm my faith, thinking of women and children
In covered wagons along the Oregon Trail,
Men on foot over Cumberland Gap;
How corruption and dishonor have always been answered
By high-hearted patriots.
Their blood runs strong in us,
A lasting part of what we are.

I have faith in the great dream of my country,
Bred to liberty at Runnymede, and nourished
By three centuries of unselfish devotion.
I believe that America is on the verge
Of something noble . . .
On the border of a new glory that shall shine
In the lives of all people everywhere.
This I believe.

Photo Opposite
GRAND TETONS
WYOMING
Bob Clemenz

They Called It America

Rabbi Abba Hillel Silver

God built him a continent of glory, and filled it with treasures untold. He studded it with sweet-flowing fountains, and traced it with long-winding streams. He carpeted it with soft-rolling prairies, and columned it with thundering mountains. He graced it with deep-shadowed forests, and filled them with song.

Then he called unto a thousand peoples, and summoned the bravest among them. They came from the ends of the earth, each bearing a gift and a hope. The glow of adventure was in their eyes, and in their hearts the glory of hope.

And out of the bounty of earth, and the labor of men; out of the longing of heart, and the prayer of souls; out of the memory of ages, and the hopes of the world, God fashioned a nation in love, and blessed it with purpose sublime.

And they called it America.

Photo Opposite
CRATER LAKE NATIONAL PAR
OREGON
Ken Dequaine

Photo Overleaf
STATUE OF LIBERTY
NEW YORK
R. Krubner
H. Armstrong Roberts, In